what do you
i can tell you
what you don't see

you don't see the girl who broke
herself loving a man who didn't care
a man who was capable of having eyes
only for me
but
chose not to

you don't see the tear soaked pillow each night
you don't see the numbers dropping on the scale
you don't see how badly it affects me

so tell me now
what do you see in her
what does she have that i don't?

aliza grace

you don't find good men at bars
you find broken ones
men you think you can fix
without taking them to bed
men who were never worthy
of getting to know you

these are the men
that will hurt you the worst

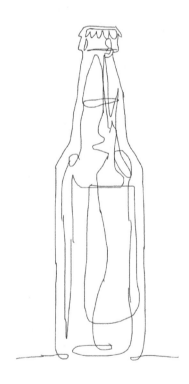

aliza grace

"please, it didn't mean anything"

then why did you do it
if it was meaningless
then why put your time and energy into cheating
why ruin our relationship
theres no coming back
from what you did
you destroyed my trust over something so
meaningless

"she does not mean anything to me, you do"

and you expect me to believe that
after throwing what we have away for another girl

infidelity

aliza grace

you watch porn
lusting after other women
when you have me

lack of intimacy

aliza grace

how can i look at you the same

knowing what you have done

knowing you broke my trust

knowing you could have stopped yourself
and didn't

you broke me

aliza grace

don't ask me for forgiveness
i am still working on forgiving myself

forgiving myself because i thought you would change

i thought you would change for me and what we had

but you didn't

and it happened again

im sorry i thought you would change

aliza grace

you were so manipulative
but i loved you
your words were so bitter towards me
but i loved you
you looked at other women outside of the relationship
but i loved you
you hurt me and i stayed
because i loved you

my love was never enough though
was it?

aliza grace

you looked into
my soul
and still lied to me

heartless

aliza grace

you cant change
a man
who doesn't
want to
change himself

aliza grace

what does she have that i don't
                                    long blonde hair
                    emerald green eyes that made you finish
                        just by looking into them long enough

i can tell you what she has
              your attention
                      it was never mine long

i don't feel special
to you
anymore
like how a partner should

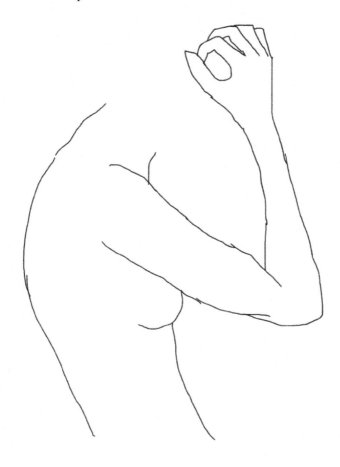

aliza grace

i wish i never met you
i wish i didn't care
i wish you didn't say you loved me
i wish you would stop calling
i wish you would disappear
i wish i wish enough for you
i wish you didn't do all the thing you've already done
i wish you cared

except these wishes
wont come true

aliza grace

my mind is dark
and filled with pain
like the black sky
before the rain
i need to let go

its ok
to have a good cry

aliza grace

7 days since it happened
why am i keeping track

        in a support group i heard its bad
        to keep track of how long ago it happened

but they say time heals
never how much time

        70 days since it happened
        and im still keeping track

        and you still cross my mind

is there enough time in my lifetime
to get over this

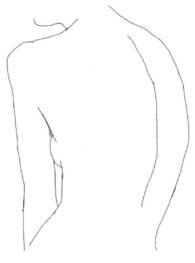

aliza grace

i deserve new skin
skin you have not gotten to touch

i deserve new lips
a mouth you have not gotten to kiss

i want to know
how it felt
touching another girl
while yours was at home

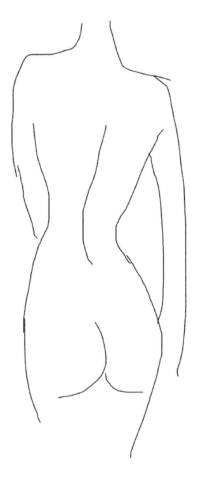

aliza grace

why are
you paying
so much
attention
to girls
who aren't
me

aliza grace

im sorry i couldn't please
you the way she did

aliza grace

i don't want things to remind me of you
because when i think of you
i think about all the horrible things you have done to me
and im thrown down a rapid hole of misery

aliza grace

if i could rewind time
i would go back to when
we were strangers

aliza grace

some days i feel everything
at once

other days i feel nothing
at all

aliza grace

i can never look at you
the same anymore
and your okay
with that

aliza grace

why didn't you
break up with me

why did you have to
go cheat on me

did it make you
feel like a man
taking off
another
womens clothes

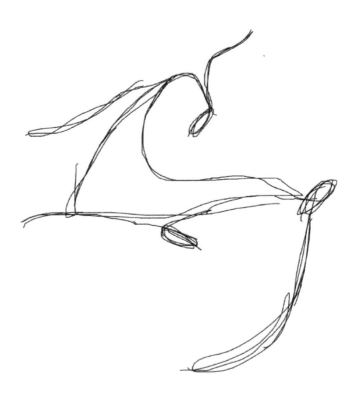

aliza grace

how can i really be with someone
who lusts after women who aren't me
who look nothing like that
how can i work twelve hour shifts
and come home to a man i cant even look in the face

im not really
here anymore

aliza grace

theres really
no room for
porn in
relationships

aliza grace

you had my heart
my mind
my soul
and
my body

so why did you need hers

aliza grace

so you got cheated on
you don't know how to feel
you start to feel everything
you blame yourself
but its not your fault
you were good enough and you know it

start blaming him

aliza grace

whats so appealing about her
why wont you tell me

aliza grace

did she do it for you
better then
i ever could

aliza grace

i hate myself
for thinking
i was enough
to make you change

theres no love in my heart
only betrayal
you will never know
how badly you hurt me
my heart is broken
in the tiniest pieces
and thrown all across the
floor

aliza grace

i would never
wish this pain
on my worst
enemy

something else that hurts
is you cant hate the girl
especially when she had no clue
you fooled us both

its you i hate

aliza grace

someone said
forgive them
and move on

i haven't even tried
to forgive you
i cant forgive you
i wont allow myself
to forgive you

you will never deserve forgiveness

aliza grace

i hope that
the next girl
you get with

does you the same way
you did to me

and i hope i cross
your mind
and your heart sinks

aliza grace

its okay
to cry

cry as long
as you need

sometimes
theres a comfort
in crying

aliza grace

some nights
i cry so much
the tears
stop coming out

aliza grace

you
never
deserved
me

aliza grace

you
broke
me
and
my
heart

aliza grace

you know
when you found out
your stomach sunk

i hate that feeling

aliza grace

im tired of being sorry
but i cant stop

sorry im not her

                                        sorry im the last pick

sorry i cant make you happy like she did

aliza grace

don't reach out
don't chase closure its not there
stay to yourself
heal what they broke
don't go back
infact never
go back

aliza grace

you deserve
someone who only
wants you

who only has eyes for you
and who loves you so much
they never want to see someone
the same way that they see you

aliza grace

your actions
spoke louder then your words

aliza grace

i cant wait till a year has past
my heart will still ache
but right now the pain
over takes my whole body
then the next thing i know im numb

say its temporary

aliza grace

i wanted all of you
i was good to you
i loved you
until you broke me

and you did
you broke me in
two

two billion pieces

im broken and you are fine

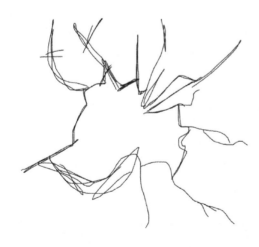

aliza grace

why
did
you
do
that
to
me

aliza grace

take my name
out of your mouth
you don't
get to
speak on it
anymore

be patient with yourself
you will never really get over it
it will just get
easier to live with

aliza grace

i don't want to
wake up in the mornings
and see your face in my head
anymore

aliza grace

erase your existence
from my mind
i don't
want to remember
you anymore

aliza grace

i want to love my body
i do
and i try each day

but

why is it so hard

aliza grace

stop making
excuses
if you really
loved me
how you say
you did
cheating would
never have crossed
your mind

aliza grace

they say
it gets worse
before it gets better

i don't think i can handle it anymore

aliza grace

crying is not gonna make him
come back to you

aliza grace

crying does not change what
he did to you

aliza grace

we
were
never
meant
to
end
like
this

aliza grace

i once loved you
a guy who was never
capable of loving me back

aliza grace

im a lot to handle
but im also a lot to lose

aliza grace

im proud
of how strong
you have been

aliza grace

not surprised
just exhausted

aliza grace

are you healed
or
do you just
try not to think about it anymore

aliza grace

ill never forget
the way you made
me feel

aliza grace

im not even sad anymore
im mad

aliza grace

you couldn't just say it was over for you
this relationship
instead you go behind my back
and lust after women who
will never look back at you

you lost the girl
who had only eyes for you

aliza grace

i forgot what a
healthy relationship feels like

in fact i never knew

aliza grace

your suppose to come to me
when you're upset
not other girls

aliza grace

the person i needed most
taught me i need nobody

<u>the art of letting go</u>
i wont answer calls from you
don't ask my friends how im doing
you don't care
i wont look at pictures
i wont listen to our music
i wont watch the movies we watched together
there will be a lot of sleepless nights
my pillow will be soaked with tears
but forgetting you
is going to feel so good

aliza grace

you said you were
sorry
but it
doesn't
feel like you are

aliza grace

shes all the thing
ill never be

aliza grace

i cant wait
to love someone new
someone who only wants just me

aliza grace

you made me
so scared
to love again

aliza grace

i want to
let go

aliza grace

maybe
human
is
not
such
a
bad
thing
to
be

you say
so ones
perfect
after
every
mistake
you make

as if that excuses you
from being a horrible person

aliza grace

im not
that hard to
love

aliza grace

aliza grace

Made in the USA
Monee, IL
04 February 2022